Take a Kid Fishing

Capt. Rob Modys

ISBN 978-1-946886-41-5

Library of Congress Control Number: 2022920831

Published by Middle River Press
Oakland Park, Florida
middleriverpress.com

First Printing—Printed in the USA

Cover Photos: Rob Modys
Photography: Rob Modys except pages 67, 69 and 70, by Debbie Hanson
Hook Chart: with permission—www.localtides.net

Take a Kid Fishing

An Adult's Guide for Introducing Youngsters
to the World of Angling

Captain Rob Modys

MIDDLE
RIVER
PRESS

Also by Captain Rob Modys

What I Know About Fishing Southwest Florida

Bridge to Paradise: Stories About Fishing, Travel, and Life

For all the kids I took fishing over the years.
Everything's better outdoors.

The mediocre teacher tells.

The good teacher explains.

The superior teacher demonstrates.

The great teacher inspires.

—William Arthur Ward

Contents

Acknowledgments

A great many kids made this book possible. Their enthusiasm and accomplishments, as they got older, inspired me to put my knowledge on paper.

I must thank the state of Florida for just being Florida. It's an amazing playground and I will be forever grateful for all the wonderful memories I have of spending time on her waters for the last sixty years or so.

To all the parents that decided to take their youngsters on a charter fishing trip and then entrusted me to entertain them, thank you. I have to admit, I learned as much from them as I hope they did from me.

My appreciation goes to all the manufactures and retailers that were kind enough to supply me with much-needed gear, especially Bass Pro Shops, Lehr's Economy Tackle, MAKO Boats, Johnson Outdoors, Power-Pole, St. Croix Rods, and Penn Reels.

To my wife, JoNell, for the initial editing, and to my publishers, Judy and Bruce of Middle River Press, for answering endless emails. You all are the best.

And finally to Todd Drew and his son Ethan, one of the many families that proved to me that taking a kid fishing is truly worth it. Ethan is holding a flounder that's almost as big as he is on the cover of this book. It was taken during a fishing charter with yours truly, just a few days before his sixth birthday at the southern end of Matlacha Pass in Lee County, Florida. I believe this was the second charter for Ethan and his dad.

One thing really stands out in my mind about those long-ago trips. Ethan, despite his young age, was already an excellent angler and could cast a bait as close to a target as just about any pro I had fished with over the years.

Ethan's fishing career began just a few years earlier when he was just three years old. Todd would take him fishing from beaches and fishing piers and said, "At that age it didn't matter what was caught, it was more about, when are we going fishing again?"

When Ethan was four, his dad bought a 16-foot center console boat that he and Ethan fished from every Sunday. They'd stop to purchase live shrimp for bait and plenty of snacks and drinks. Todd says he never made Ethan stay out on the water any longer than he wanted to. However, most trips ended when they ran out of shrimp or it was getting late and time to return to the boat ramp.

Ethan hooked up with his first tarpon at the age of four. Unfortunately he had set his rod down to grab a snack, so the tarpon took his rod right out of the boat—lesson learned.

Todd Drew began his fishing addiction in freshwater mountain streams for brook, rainbow, and brown trout with his grandfathers when he was five years old. They both enjoyed fishing so they would take him along. His dad didn't care much for fishing, but he bought a small Jon boat with a nine-horsepower motor that he would use to take Todd fishing on the local ponds.

When Ethan was eight years old he and his father began saltwater tournament fishing. Todd said, "He caught the bug badly!" He continued, "We would fish every tournament that we could." It's important to note that Ethan was also playing soccer and baseball on a regular basis, but the pair still continued to fish tournaments.

Ethan began talking about becoming a fishing guide when he was in high school. After graduation he attended Florida Gulf Coast University, but after only one year decided to go into business for himself—as a fishing guide. He started the process of getting his captain's license and the other credentials needed to legally ply the waters as a guide in Florida.

I'm proud to say that Captain Ethan Drew now has his own charter business, Drewitup Charters, based out of Fort Myers, Florida.

Foreword

In 1948 my first fishing gear was a cane pole with line, a bobber, a hook, and a worm. I grew up in Momence, Illinois, a small farm town fifty miles south of Chicago. A river ran through it—the Kankakee. It was my playground and a source of my fondest memories. My older brother, Bob, and I spent our summer days fishing for carp with homemade dough-balls and targeted smallmouth bass with creek chubs. At night we used stinky cheese to catch catfish. During the winter afternoons we'd head to the east-side quarry to ice-fish and spent springtime days catching crappie behind the dam.

My dad loved to fish, so family vacations usually meant a fishing trip. When I was nine he would drive the family down to Florida on old US 41 where we fished for seatrout near Tampa and then spent time at the beach near Fort Myers going after sheepshead. The next year we went to Escanaba, Michigan, to fish for walleye.

I fished as often as possible no matter where I was. Time was spent in Wisconsin, Florida, and Texas, but eventually I wound up in manufacturing management for forty-five years, and fishing fell by the wayside. My father, who had introduced me to fishing, would often invite me to join him for salmon trips on Lake Michigan, but I seldom took him up on his offers. He would say, "Bud, you work too hard. Take time to go fishing." I wish I had taken his advice many years ago.

When the time for retirement arrived my wife, Linda, was adamant that we find a place where I could fish. Southwest Florida, with its reputation for some of the best fishing in the country, fit the bill. At 70 years of age I bought a place in Naples in a gated community called Windstar. One of its main attractions was the fact that it has 22 lakes scattered around a golf course. It also happened to have a newly formed Windstar Fishing Club.

Five years passed and I became the president of the club. One of my tasks was to find guest speakers for our meetings and that's where I met Captain Rob Modys. He was one of our best speakers and was helpful in recommending other local fishing guides for future speaking engagements with our group.

Captain Rob's first book, *What I Know About Fishing Southwest Florida*, is brilliant—filled with color photos and personal stories and sprinkled with humor. It is based on Captain Rob's reliance on science and his years of experience as an inshore guide. It is the most complete and helpful book on how to catch local fish that has ever been written. When a newcomer to Southwest Florida asks how to learn to fish in this area, I tell them to join a fishing club, hire a good guide, and read Captain Rob's book.

The fishing club has grown from 40 members to over 100, which includes 35 women. After six years as president I turned over the reins of leadership, but retained the responsibility for the "Take a Windstar Grandkid Fishing" program, which had become my personal passion.

What started small rapidly grew into something much bigger than expected. When residents asked if I'd give instruction to visiting grandchildren I said yes, but had to set a few ground rules and guidelines to make sure adult participation and safety was assured.

Over the last four years we've provided instruction and fishing to over three-hundred kids on the Windstar lakes. There have been some amazing catches with a lot of great stories and memories made.

You hold in your hands *Take A Kid Fishing, An Adult's Guide for Introducing Youngsters to the World of Angling*. It's a wealth of information about what it takes to give kids the confidence to take on the sport of fishing and hopefully teach them to become responsible future anglers. Captain Rob has once again shared his knowledge in hopes that you will share this with kids you know and get them out of the house and into the great outdoors.

Take my father's advice. Take the time to go fishing and pass it on.

Clyde Torp
Windstar Fishing Club

Introduction

I started fishing when I was six years old. My dad took me to the pier in Clearwater, Florida, where I caught my very first saltwater fish. Well, not really. The first thing I caught that day was not technically a fish; it was an octopus. I remember the excitement it caused the other fishermen, when it squirted purple ink everywhere but managed to miss all of us.

With the help of fellow anglers the octopus was unhooked and returned safely to the water.

This surprising event was the beginning of my fishing addiction.

I'm now in my late sixties, yet the wonder of what might bite when I cast a line in the water has never waned. I've fished in some amazing places from Scotland to the Bahamas and a great many places across the United States. I've made a career of angling as a fishing guide, radio show and podcast host and in years of teaching fishing classes, all because my father took the time to take me fishing that very first time.

Taking a kid fishing is important. It teaches them lifelong lessons about the great outdoors, conservation, and sportsmanship. It introduces them to an abundance of wildlife, fascinating adventures and an endearing community of fishing friends. It solidifies a bond between parent and child that I believe can't be underestimated. While on a fishing trip there are no outside distractions from the internet, video games, and movies. It's a time for conversation and bonding between you, the child, and the great outdoors.

A song called *Just Fishin'*, written by Casey Beathard, Monty Criswell, and Ed Hill and sung by country music artist Trace Adkins, is about taking a young daughter fishing and how she thinks they are "just fishing," while in reality, so much more is happening. Memories and bonds will form that will never be forgotten. That's why taking a youngster fishing is so important.

The idea for this book started in the early 2000s when I began my charter fishing career. At first I fished the very experienced hardcore anglers.

Every once in a while they'd bring a son, daughter or both along for the trip. As time went by I began to be known as a teaching captain, especially with youngsters, and that prompted parents to look me up based on word-of-mouth recommendations from friends and relatives.

I still continued to take the big guns fishing for snook, redfish, and tarpon, but my focus changed over time to families. They were much more interested in quantity of action for their youngsters versus how big and how rare a catch might be. Experienced fishing guides will tell you that it's easy to catch a lot of fish but difficult to find numbers of highly sought-after species. Keep this in mind when fishing with kids.

This book is about how to successfully take kids fishing and what I learned over the years fishing alongside them on a charter boat. The information is Florida-based with a mix of saltwater and freshwater advice, but can easily be adapted to other areas that have freshwater lakes, ponds, and streams.

Fishing is not only a sport, it's also a tradition that's handed down almost entirely from family member to family member and friend to friend. For me it began as far back as my great-grandfather. Hopefully this book will help parents, grandparents, friends, and relatives make the step to ensure that every kid gets a chance to go fishing. It's a sport that builds life-long friendships and memories. Fishing gets kids out in nature and helps them discover who they are as people.

I signed off every one of my radio shows by saying "please take a kid fishing." That's my advice to you—and remember, it's not just fishing.

Capt. Rob Modys
Key Largo, Florida
2022

Basic Tips

Let me start with this. When fishing with children, especially young children, the event is all about them. To truly get a kid hooked on fishing you will have to forego some of the catching you would normally take part in when fishing by yourself or with close adult friends. The more focus you put on the child, the more likely the experience will be fun and rewarding for them, and they will continue to want to go fishing.

Have An Answer For Everything

Just about every child I took fishing during my career as a charter boat captain loved the experience. They all seemed to have a never-ending curiosity about what was happening around them, and they proved it by constantly asking questions, not only about fishing, but about everything within eyesight. "What kind of boat is this?" "What kind of boat is that?" "Was that a dolphin or a manatee?" "What is that big white bird called?"

Be prepared, because this inquisitiveness will go on throughout the entire fishing learning experience, and children will ask the same questions over and over again. Hang in there; patience is a virtue for which you will be richly rewarded.

Most kids under eight years of age have a very short attention span, especially boys. I know of what I speak of because I raised all girls. My brother raised a girl and two boys and I watched them grow up, so I was able to observe and compare. Girls tend to self-entertain while boys need almost constant input from other sources. When you are on a fishing trip, whether it's on a boat or along a shore, you'll be the continuous source of input.

I bought a dollhouse for my youngest daughter when she was about five years old. It came complete with furniture, bath and kitchen fixtures, and a car, bicycle, cat, dog, siblings, and parents. She would sit for hours and make up stories about the family while rearranging the entire house to suit the stories.

Boys, on the other hand, will switch the toys they are playing with almost constantly. Yes, they'll get attached to some longer than others, but more often than not they'll lose interest and head off to find something else to do. That can be a big problem while spending several hours on a boat that's eighteen feet long and only seven feet wide.

How Young Is Too Young?

The most common question I received from potential charter customers about fishing with children was minimum age limitations. In my opinion most children are able to start fishing at around five years of age. That includes both boys and girls. While boys seem to be more interested in fishing at a younger age, I can assure you that girls have the skills to start young too. Girls are also more likely to catch more fish early on in the process due to the fact that they pay closer attention to details than boys do at younger ages.

Keep this in mind. If you enjoy fishing and being outdoors, please impart that to your kids, male or female, at an early age. As they grow up they'll develop into great fishing partners and there's nothing better for communication between parent and child than spending time together in the uncluttered outdoors.

Short Attention Span Theater

For the younger kids be sure to bring other things for them to do while on a boat or at the beach or lake. Most younger children will fish almost constantly for about an hour or two at the most, so you'll either need to complete the trip early or you'll need to give them a break. My charters normally were a half day, or about four hours. When the children began to wane I'd suggest looking for dolphins or perhaps a stop at a beach to hunt for shells. The same applies for shore fishing. You'll need to provide creative alternatives during the down times.

Charter Trips With Kids

Here are some important tips. If you decide to take your kids on a fishing charter please understand that the captain's focus will mostly be on the child and not you. That means as the adult you may at times have to bait

Sheepshead are fairly easy to find in the fall and winter
months along Southwest Florida's coast.

your own hook, retrieve your catch from the water, and perhaps untangle
a bird's nest of fishing line from your reel. One thing is for sure. If the kids
are happy you'll have more time to fish. Charter captains will do their best
to keep kids happy.

Fishing is fun. One of things I learned from a young angler was the
game of "how many" and "how big." It's simple to play. Have the kid(s)
keep track of what they've caught. In some cases scores are applied to each
species of fish. The more unusual a catch, the more points are scored. Of
course this is entirely subject to opinion and some rules can be changed

mid-game. I have even had kids that applied negative scores to undesir-able catches. Add up the score at the end of the trip and you have the winner.

Lastly, never ever yell or show disappointment if a young angler has a fail moment. Fishing is not a competitive field sport like soccer, baseball, or football, and I've witnessed some terrible adult behavior at ball parks. Yelling at a child for a missed opportunity doesn't work. Teaching them sportsmanship does. There will be many mistakes including lost big fish, lures in the bushes, broken rods, and hook sets that just don't get the job done. Even seasoned anglers have these same bad moments. Please do your absolute best to not show disappointment, but instead use these situations to give encouragement when coaching young anglers.

Fishing Regulations

Fishing regulations vary from state to state in the U.S. The rules included here apply only to Florida and can quickly change throughout the year. Even though the Florida Fish and Wildlife Conservation Commission (FWC) addresses fishing regulations quarterly, they may also implement emergency regulations at any time. It's a good idea to set up notifications from the FWC's email or from an online application so you can be informed of changes if and when they occur. The same is true for most other states. When it comes to fishing rules you can't have too much information. Keep in mind that it's always on the angler's shoulders to know the current rules before heading out for a day of fishing.

At this writing a fishing license for either saltwater or freshwater is not required for any child under 16 years of age while fishing in the state of Florida. This rule also applies to out-of-state children that are visiting. However, all other rules such as season closures, size limits, and bag limits still apply to all anglers.

Florida has an absolute ton of regulated fish species. You name the fish and it most likely has rules for open and closed seasons, bag limits, size limits, and proper measuring techniques. It's important that you pass this knowledge along to youngsters. They need to know what these rules are and what they mean for the future of Florida's fisheries.

I personally have no problem with keeping legally caught fish, but teaching the value of catch and release should be a part of educating young anglers. The more fish that are released, the more there will be to catch in the future.

Safe Handling

When handling fish for measurements or photos, be sure to include the child in the process. Have them learn how to properly net and land a fish, whether alongside the boat, at the beach, or lakeshore.

Teach them the importance of wetting their hands before touching fish, especially if the fish is going to be released. Using a towel, shirt or dry hands to hold a fish can remove the natural slime coating. The sliminess is very important in keeping waterborne parasites from attaching to the skin of the fish after release back into the water.

Try not to hold fish by the jaw, and always support the belly of medium- to larger-sized fish while handling before they are released. Their internal organs aren't designed to be out of the water so the extra gravity can tear or damage them.

If you are going to harvest the fish for food be sure to have an adequate cooler full of ice nearby. Fish can spoil quickly so it's best to get them into ice as soon as possible.

Kid's Safety

Kids will be kids, especially on a boat, at the beach, and at the lake. They honestly love being in the great outdoors. I'm guessing it is the fresh air that enhances their activity to a level that's hard to comprehend. I've often thought how wonderful it would be if someone could come up with a way to bottle that energy so that grownups could have a dose every now and then. I used to tell parents that after four hours of fishing their youngsters were going to need a nice long nap. They'd usually smile after hearing this.

Lifejackets

Most U.S. states require some sort of wearable floatation device for children and adults when onboard a boat, kayak, or canoe. In the state of Florida a United States Coast Guard (USCG)-approved wearable lifejacket is mandatory for children under the age of six while underway on any vessel less than twenty-six feet in length. Please note the "underway" wording in this rule. You may remove the lifejacket from the child, if you wish, when the boat motor has been fully shut down. Anytime the motor is running, the USCG considers the boat as being underway and the child needs to be wearing the lifejacket.

I mention the underway rule for the unseen advantage it has for youngsters that will be fishing. It's easier for them to handle a fishing rod without the encumbrance of a rather bulky USCG-approved lifejacket. However, if the child does not know how to swim, and as a parent or guardian you feel that they could possibly fall into the water, then by all means leave the lifejacket on. Safety first.

Keep in mind that guardians also have the option of switching the USCG-approved jacket for children to a low-profile ski vest while the boat is shut down for fishing. These life vests are made specifically for outdoor sports and fishing, and offer unencumbered mobility for casting and reeling. They also are sold in small sizes for children.

Hydration

Kids have a tendency to not drink enough of anything, especially water, while fishing. This becomes an even bigger problem during the hot summer months. The activity and concentration of fishing seems to blur their need for hydration. Adults need to keep a close eye on them for signs of heat exhaustion. It comes on quickly with children and it's the last thing you want to have to deal with on a boat.

As a boat captain I made it a habit of recommending water at regular intervals and also looking for signs of dehydration that aren't all that difficult to spot. Cheeks and foreheads will begin to flush pink and then red, and then the typical childlike activity—talking and inquisitiveness—will slow way down. When this is noted the quickest thing to do is make the child drink water right away and then head toward the dock as quickly as you can. Sometimes the boat ride will provide enough breeze to cool them down more quickly. Remember, this is a serious situation and should be handled as such. If the child become listless on the way to the dock, dial 911 immediately and have them meet you at your planned destination.

Sun Protection

Sunblock is essential for all outdoor activities, especially fishing, due to the lack of access to cover or shade from the sun on some watercraft. Shade can also be lacking when at the beach or alongside a lake if a beach umbrella or sun tent isn't available.

I recommend applying a 45 to 50 SPF lotion-type sunblock before leaving the house or hotel room. Cooler skin holds the sunblock better than sweaty, hot skin and that will help increase the time between the first dose and repeated applications. Light-colored boat decks readily reflect the sun upward, even under large brimmed hats, so be sure to apply sunblock under chins and on the backs of legs.

I'm not a big fan of sunblock sprays, but I know they are used quite often by parents for easily coating their kids. A problem occurs when this type of sunblock is applied or reapplied on a boat. The overspray makes the deck very slippery. For this reason and for everyone's safety it's best to use lotions instead of spays when boating.

I've worn sunblock for a good part of my life, especially during my professional stint as a charter captain, so believe me, lotion works better. It stays on the skin longer despite sweat and swimming, and offers overall better protection from the sun when applied before going outside.

Be sure to also supply a hat that fits the child well and has a large all-around brim to protect the youngster's face and shoulders. The extra shade will also help to cut down on the heat from the sun. There are also coverups and shirts available that have built-in SPF. They may cost a little more, but are certainly worth it for sun protection in the long run.

Hooks and Knives

This is simple common sense. Keep sharp stuff away from children. This can easily be overlooked on a boat that has been mostly occupied by adults for fishing. The child is brought along for an outing, but knives are still in holders around the console or near the bait well. Be sure to stow them in a safe place before the fishing trip begins and also after the knives have been used to cut bait, etc.

Hooks are meant for fish not kids. Keep this in mind for the entire fishing trip and things should go well. One step I take, even when adults are fishing, is mashing down the barbs on treble hooks. These hooks are a menace and I've seen way too many instances of severe hookups with humans. Removing a barbed hook from skin is no fun for the remover or for the patient, so do both a favor by flattening the barbs of the hooks with a pair of fishing pliers. It's simple and will save a fishing trip by not having to make a run to the emergency room.

Distractions

This is directed toward the adults. Stay off the cellphone except to take photographs. Please keep a close eye on your kids when they are on a boat, dock, beach, or lakeside. I've seen a lot of close calls and I've even snatched a child out of the water after she fell overboard. Kids move quickly. Always be aware of where they are and what they are doing or about to do.

Try to avoid walking behind a child when they are actively fishing. Even though I've instructed youngsters to always look behind themselves before casting, this tip is soon forgotten in the heat of battle.

Kids have a tendency to yank a fish out of the water as quickly as possible when it's close to the boat, dock, or shoreline. The weight of the fish increases as it's lifted out of the water and this can cause the hook, jig head or lure to pop out of the mouth and then ricochet in about three different directions all at once. Careful and constant coaching will help nip this habit in the bud. I tell young anglers to keep the fish in the water so that it won't unhook itself. This usually gets their attention because no one wants to lose a fish. Grab the net and scoop up the fish before extra tension can be placed on the fishing line.

Basic Fishing Gear for Kids

There's an abundance of "kiddie" rod and reel combos on the market. They are available just about everywhere fishing equipment is sold. OK, they're cute and have Superman, Batman, and Little Mermaid on them, but let's get serious about this. Those combos may get some interest from youngsters under the age of five or six, but for first graders and up it's much better to start them off with something that you might fish with, but on a slightly smaller scale. All children like to be treated like they are much older than they are, so an adult-like fishing rod and reel is a very big deal to them.

This little gal is ready for the big one! Note the rod flotation device in front of her hand. If she loses the rod overboard it will float.

Rods

For physically smaller children, do your best to find a rod that's about five-and-a-half feet long. You can go up a bit, but stay on the short side if you can. When it comes to bigger kids, they can most certainly handle a rod that's six to seven feet in length. In both cases the long rods may seem difficult to use at first, but don't worry; kids tend to adapt quickly.

Be sure to involve the child in the purchase. Have them hold several rods so they can feel the difference between each one, and let them help in the decision making. If a combo rod and reel purchase is not being made, make sure to add a reel to the rod being considered so that the proper balance can be felt.

If fishing is going to be done in both fresh and saltwater you'll need to invest in a saltwater rod. The cost will be slightly higher, but it will last much longer. Salt is very corrosive and no matter how well you clean a freshwater rod it will soon degrade and rust.

What to spend is the big question. A decently constructed rod can be purchased from about forty dollars upward. I usually recommend spending somewhere in the vicinity of eighty dollars. But again, the cost decision needs to be made by the adult. You most likely know your child or grandchild better than most and you'll also have a good feel for how enthused the youngster will be about this new endeavor. Rest assured that if he or she falls in love with the sport, they will most certainly want to upgrade as time passes.

Reels

The reel should be somewhat smaller and lighter than what an adult would use. Stay away from metal if you can and instead go with graphite. It's lighter in weight and more durable. A lighter reel can also be used much longer during a fishing trip by a youngster. The longer a little person can fish, the more likely they'll catch fish and be motivated to stick with it.

In most cases it's a good idea to start kids off with the classic Zebco Spincast closed-face reel. They were the first reels used by a lot of us adult anglers, and they still work well for children. Again, if saltwater is in the mix check out Zebco's Saltfisher line of Spincast reels.

If this will be their first rod and reel, there's nothing wrong with keeping the expenses down until you see signs that they have been bitten by the fishing bug.

Fishing Line

When it comes to fishing line the two most popular choices are monofilament and braid. Both work well, but for kids I'd highly recommend starting them off with braid if possible. Braided line doesn't stretch or twist and is less likely to foul or become tangled. Braid is also more sensitive because of the lack of stretch, and that enables youngsters to better feel the bite. I'm not saying that monofilament line doesn't work. What I am saying is that braid is easier for kids to use when they are learning to fish.

Go with a brightly colored fishing line such as high-vis yellow or light blue. These colors make it easier to see where the fishing line is while a lure or bait is in the water. This is especially important when fishing in saltwater where tides create currents of moving water that will push the line in unknown directions.

Lastly, start with fifteen- to twenty-pound test braided line. If mono is used, go with eight- to ten-pound test.

Another thing to keep in mind is that braid has a bit of buoyancy and will stay closer to the surface of the water. Monofilament, on the other hand, sinks. I believe that the ability to see where the line is after the cast is important when teaching kids to fish. It also helps them learn how well they are able to direct a cast to a specific location.

Leader Line

A leader of either monofilament or fluorocarbon is needed for saltwater fishing, but not always for freshwater. As a matter of fact most freshwater anglers just tie hooks and lures directly to the main fishing line. However, a great many species of saltwater fish are very line shy so there's a need for extra stealth. I tend to side with fluorocarbon vs. monofilament leader because it's virtually invisible in water.

Currently there are two thoughts about fluorocarbon color. That's right; just like everything else in the world of fishing, many variables come into play. Fluorocarbon is available in clear and pink. It would seem that the way to go would obviously be the clear line, but there is proof that the pink somehow works better in clearer water.

Here's what I found from a test of my own. Clear fluorocarbon casts a shadow when sunlight hits it from above. Pink does not. Pink also seems to diffuse light better at depth. When snorkeling with a piece of both the clear and the pink, it was noticeable that the pink leader was much more difficult to see in about five feet of water. Honestly, I have no idea why this is true, but I personally changed to pink leader several years ago.

Another reason to use fluorocarbon leaders is they protect the standing fishing line from abrasion and bite-offs. Fluorocarbon is not only invisible in water, but it's also tougher. I actually started adding it to my freshwater rigs several years ago when fishing for invasive species in South Florida. Those fish sometimes have teeth and sharp gill plates, and fight very much like saltwater fish. They have a bad habit of looking for obstructions to use to abrade and cut fishing line. When it comes to young anglers I'd recommend using it for both fresh and saltwater. After all, keeping fish hooked and landed for kids is a good thing.

Tackle Box

Be sure to purchase the child their very own tackle box or bag. This is the number one accessory item that children ask for when they begin fishing. A tackle box gives kids the feeling of being real fishermen with their own collection of lures and supplies. It will help them begin to make decisions on what to use during certain situations, and this becomes a great learning tool as they begin to spend more time fishing.

A tackle bag or box will also give you endless gift selection possibilities as the holidays and birthdays come and go, and once the first one is filled another tackle bag will have to be added. I guess you see where this is going.

Basic Fishing Tackle for Kids

In the beginning keep things as simple as possible. I'd recommend starting with hooks, small weights, bobbers, and popping corks.

Fishing Hooks

Hooks are a tad complicated partly because of the introduction of the circle hook to saltwater fishing in the mid 1990s. I find it strange that it took modern anglers and fishing tackle manufactures a very long time to catch on to a hook that was created centuries ago by the native Maori of New Zealand. Similar circle-shaped bone hooks have also been found in many archaeological sites throughout the Pacific islands.

Their popularity was slow moving here in the United States, but once anglers began to understand how to use a circle hook correctly the popularity grew rapidly. It's important to understand that unlike a standard J-hook, an angler doesn't need to set the hook when the strike or nibble of a fish is felt when fishing with a circle hook. Instead the line is tightened by reeling and the hook essentially sets itself. For older anglers that were taught to jerk the end of the fishing rod with every bite, this new approach of NOT setting a hook seemed almost impossible to master. I was one of those. It took me quite a long while to readapt, but when I did I began to catch and land more fish.

Circle hooks are a blessing for kids just learning how to fish. Because they've never been taught how to set a hook they'll do what comes naturally. When they feel a bite or see a bobber disappear from the surface of the water, they'll simply reel in the line. In most cases that's a caught fish, and the more fish that are landed the more likely you've created a new angler for life. With kids it's good to remember it's a numbers game—how many and not necessarily how big.

In both salt and freshwater, hook sizes used are relatively the same. When baitfishing, go with small hooks for small fish species with small mouths, and slightly larger hooks for bigger fish with bigger mouths.

Fishing Hook Size Guide

8   7   6   5   4   3   2   1

1/0   2/0   3/0   4/0   5/0   6/0   7/0   8/0

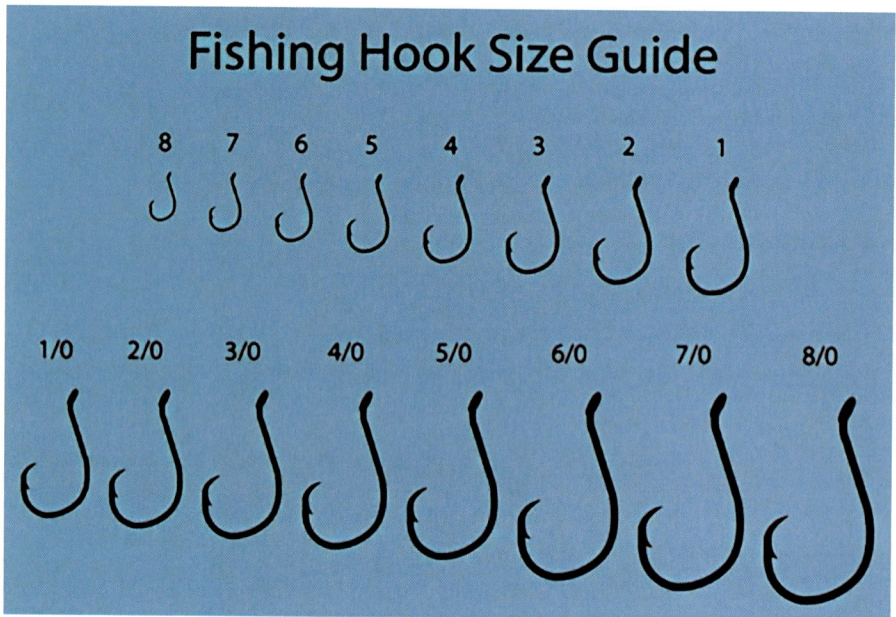

Hook sizing for fishing is a bit unusual. I've provided a simple chart to explain.

On the upper line of the chart whole numbers are used for hook sizes. A size 8 hook is very small and sizes 7 through 1 are larger. Moving to the bottom row of the chart, oughts are used for hook sizes. A small hook in this case would be 1/0 and a very large hook would be the 8/0. If you were to put the two lines together in one long row, a number 1 hook is only slightly smaller than a 1/0 hook. Confusing? You bet.

Simply put, the normal range of hook sizes that will be used for the represented fish targets in this book should run from a number 2 up to a 3/0.

Fishing Weights

Fishing weights are attached to terminal tackle to help get hooked live or frozen baits near or all-the-way down to the the bottom. When current is present from either tides or winds it might be necessary to add weight to keep offerings in the target zone.

When weights are needed while teaching kids to fish, I'd recommend going mostly with split shots. They are small, round weights with a slot cut in them where the fishing line or leader line is placed. You then squeeze the weight shut with fishing pliers. They are available in a multitude of sizes, and once again the numbering system is a bit confusing. A No. 1 split shot is larger than a No. 13. The most commonly used sizes for both saltwater and freshwater fishing are 7's, 5's and 3's. They are simple to use, so a child can easily master moving or removing them with a pair of fishing pliers. Look for split shots that come with small wings, so that they can be easily reopened for repositioning them on the leader or fishing line.

Just a thought: Fishing pliers would make a nice addition to a young angler's tackle box.

Bobbers and Popping Corks

There's a notable difference between bobbers and popping corks. Bobbers are generally used while fishing in freshwater ponds and lakes, while popping corks are mostly used in saltwater. While both signal to the angler that a fish is taking a bait, the popping cork also works as a fish attractor. As its name suggests, the popping cork is designed to create noise, specifically a sound that resembles a fish attacking small baitfish that are schooling near the surface of the water.

I have used them successfully while freshwater fishing in Florida, but mainly as a bite indicator, and not so much as a noise maker. However, they are absolutely essential for saltwater fishing and I wouldn't go angling without them in my tackle bag.

Kids and adults both love popping corks, not only because they are visual bite indicators, but because they can greatly relieve the boredom of a slow bite. They need to be constantly worked in order to work. Let me explain.

The popping cork is slightly weighted on the bottom so that it floats perpendicular to the water. The top is cupped and the bottom rounded. The fishing line is attached to the top, and the leader line us attached to the bottom along with a hook or jig head. After casting, the angler gives the rod a sharp pull which causes the scalloped top to scoop up water and creates a sound similar to the sound gamefish make when busting a bait near the water's surface. I call it "ringing the dinner bell." Nearby fish hear the sound and are attracted to it because they think (I believe that fish can think) that one of their compadres is getting something that they would also like to eat.

The two photos are examples of popping cork rigs. On the left is the more common circle hook and split-shot rig, good for live baitfish or shrimp. On the right is a jig head rig, great for live shrimp rigged by the tail. The jig provides the weight, so no split shot is needed.

When it comes to kids, the popping cork can be a boredom reliever. It also helps to get them prepped and accustomed to using artificial lures. While a popping cork can be simply watched as a bite indicator, making noise with it is what makes it special, and kids love to make it pop. I can't begin to tell you how excited they get when the popping pays off with an attack from a fish and a disappearing cork.

Sometimes a surprise takes the bait. Permit are rarely caught in inshore waters and are a prized fish for all anglers.

Live and Frozen Bait for Saltwater

I believe that the easiest way to get fish to bite in fresh or saltwater is with the use of live baits. I personally love artificials and I also fly fish, but I know a thing or two about getting lots of bites from lots of fish. There are a great many live and frozen baits that can be purchased from bait shops and tackle dealers, especially near the areas you're hoping to go fishing. Frozen baits are a very close second choice, and are in most cases easier to come by, but do your best to find the live goodies if possible. I'll explain why in this chapter.

Live and Frozen Shrimp

For saltwater fishing the easiest and most effective bait is live shrimp. It's available at just about every coastal bait and tackle shop in Florida. It's usually sold by the dozen and often has pricing discounts for larger quantities. Just make sure to buy enough. When it comes to kids you do NOT want to run out of bait during a fishing trip. How much is enough? Take the following into account when purchasing live shrimp.

It's not always necessary to use the whole live shrimp when baiting kid's hooks. Depending on size, a single shrimp can be broken in half, or sometimes into three pieces. This almost always leads to discussions of what makes the better bait, the head, middle, or tail. Kids love to keep track of everything numbers-wise on a fishing trip, so take advantage of this and even you, the adult, might learn which part of the shrimp is the best. I'm still not sure.

Kids burn through shrimp in a hurry, especially if they are just starting out in the sport of fishing. It sometimes takes awhile for them to react to feeling or seeing (under a bobber) the bite. That's where breaking the bait into smaller portions helps quite a bit. On initial trips I would recommend at least twenty-five to thirty shrimp per child.

Remember, live shrimp is preferred; however, frozen will work in a pinch and makes a good backup plan if you do run out of live shrimp. However, frozen shrimp softens quickly when thawing and is more likely to fall apart when casting, so extra care has to be used when putting it on a hook. Keeping as much of the outer shell as possible on the shrimp while placing it on the hook will help quite a bit.

Frozen also tends to attract more saltwater catfish and strange bottom dwellers which aren't high on the list of the most wanted species. However, in the early stages of fishing kids don't usually care too much about what they've hooked up with on the end of the line, just so long as it's pulling and fighting. Catfish fight well, but catfish also come with nasty spines that will sting. A child getting poked can mess up a perfectly good fishing trip, so be careful during the release. Yes, live shrimp will also get eaten by catfish, but much less so than the frozen version.

Be sure to take advantage of teaching the young angler how to bait their own hook. Not only is it an important step in learning how to fish, but it also imparts independence and will free you, the teacher, to possibly do a little fishing too. Teach them how to net a shrimp from a live well or bucket and how to safely handle live shrimp. Show them the rostrum, the horn at the tip of the head, and also the spike at the center of the tail, called the telson. None of these sharp points are all that dangerous and rarely draw blood, but they can prick young skin a little more easily than adults.

There are two basic ways to put shrimp on a hook. The first is running the hook sideways through the rostrum. This works well because it keeps the shrimp very much alive and the toughness of the rostrum helps keep the hook in place. The second way requires the removal of the tail and then running the hook up through the meat and out through bottom of the shrimp near the legs. This is very effective when using lead jig heads with live shrimp.

Frozen Squid

If live or frozen shrimp are unavailable, go to the dark side and buy frozen squid. It's also attractive to catfish and other bottom feeders, but is readily eaten by a host of other saltwater fish. I specifically used it when taking kids fishing for mangrove snapper, which happen to be plentiful and fantastic bait stealers. Their ability to suck bait off a hook in mere seconds can frustrate young kids in short order. Frozen squid cut into small thin strips can be put on a hook by threading the point of the hook through the meat several times. Squid is tough and snapper have a hard time getting all the bait at once. This will lead to more hookups and happier kids.

There are several steps needed to prepare frozen squid for placement on a hook. First, thaw and then remove the head and tentacles by pulling them away from the tube shaped body. Next, remove the entrails and the clear quill (cartilage plate) in the center of the squid body. What's left is a whitish-colored tube that looks similar to a windsock seen at airports. Place it on a cutting board and begin cutting quarter-inch slices from the largest end until you get to the tip of the cone. These will be rings of squid, the same type that is cooked for calamari! Cut each of the rings open so that what remains is a long strip of squid a quarter-inch wide. The strip can easily be threaded onto the hook. Make sure to leave about half of the strip dangling from the end of the hook. Snapper can't resist this wavy worm-like presentation. Once you've cut the squid strips, remember to put the knife away and out of reach.

Frozen Mullet

Often referred to as frozen finger mullet, these small, oily fish usually come three to five per package. You'll need to thaw them for fishing. I like to do that slowly, one at a time, so that they don't become mushy in the heat of the day. Cut them in chunks about a half-inch thick and rig them on a circle hook with a split-shot weight added above the hook. This is a favorite of mine for fishing the nearshore rock piles and wrecks for snapper and grunts. It gives off a smell that only a fish could love. This is also my go-to for shark fishing.

Searching for seatrout sometimes leads to the best kind of surprise catch.
A redfish!

Freshwater Baits

One word. Worms. More specifically, night crawlers or earthworms. They are available at bait shops and are sold in small containers full of muddy dirt. The entire worm can be threaded onto a hook, or they can be used by cutting them into smaller pieces. I usually cut them when going after bluegill and small cichlids, but leave them whole for largemouth bass.

Depending on where you live and the type of soil you have, night crawlers can be caught by hand instead of being purchased. It's best to hunt for them at night when they tend to come up out of the soil, but you can also look under things like stepping stones, drainage splash blocks and old boards lying on the ground. Searching for them after an evening rain is also good, and some folks will turn on sprinklers at night to bring them up out of the ground. No matter the method, kids love hunting for them, so be sure to get them involved.

Rigging for worms is pretty simple. Put as much of a whole or partial worm as you can layer onto a circle hook. The fish will try to inhale the whole thing at once, and all the child has to do is crank the handle of the reel.

Use bobber rigs when teaching younger kids, especially those that are just starting to learn to fish. Place the worm on a circle hook rigged about eighteen inches or so under a bobber. It's a good idea to also add a split-shot weight just a few inches above the hook. This will help keep the bait down in the strike zone. If there's a bit of current or a breeze across the surface of the water, it would be advisable to add a larger, heavier split shot. Again, this will help keep the bait in the target zone, especially during a drift. Make sure the bobber can be moved up and down the line so the depth of the presentation can be easily adjusted. This is important because fish tend to eat in a specific depth range, and this can change from day to day depending on conditions. If there are no bites after floating a bait in a fishy looking area for five or ten minutes, it may be time to reset the depth. I've seen anglers pick up and move without doing depth adjustments only to have someone else come in behind them minutes later, cast a worm and bobber combo in the same, area and down goes the bobber.

Shiners

These small baitfish are sold by the dozen at bait shops. Simply put, big fish eat little fish and shiners are little silvery colored fish. They can be free-lined on a hook with no weight, or suspended under a bobber just like worms. The only drawback is their cost. A dozen shiners can be expensive, so keep that in mind when kids are first learning how to fish. The early learning days equals lots of lost baits.

Even though shiners are preferred by most seasoned anglers, it's probably best to start with worms from a cost-effective standpoint. When you think your child is ready, then give the shiners a shot.

Crickets and Grasshoppers

These can also be purchased at bait stores, although crickets are much more common. Terrestrial baits are most often used for catching panfish in the spring when warm temperatures and spring rain brings about hatches of bugs alongside creeks, ponds and lakes. A good rain shower will wash these little critters into the water. When it comes to taking kids fishing for bluegill, sunfish, and shell crackers in the spring and summer, it's hard to beat a cricket for bait.

Drawbacks? Some kids are afraid of bugs and don't want to touch them, much less put them on a hook.

Artificial Lures for Saltwater

First and foremost, here's a safety tip for the use of artificial lures when used by children and in most cases with adults too. Be sure to flatten down the hook barbs. This will make removing a hook from human skin much easier if the unexpected happens.

The barb of a fishing hook is the small appendage near the tip of the hook that helps hold the hook in place while fighting a fish. It will do the same if it penetrates human skin. However, human skin is much tougher than that of most fish, so it's quite difficult and painful to remove a hook that has entered the skin deep enough to go past the barb. Flattening, or mashing down the barb, is easy to do and will make releasing a human much easier. A pair of needle-nose pliers is all that's needed to take care of the barb, and in no way will this affect the integrity of the hook itself.

My general rule is to remove the barbs only on artificial lures that have the more typical treble hooks. A great many of these same lures have at least two trebles, and sometimes three. As mentioned, the barb is designed to help hold the hook in the mouth of a fish. I honestly believe that most anglers, even children, will have a hard time losing a hooked fish with at least three hooks in the mouth.

Lead-Head Jigs

Jigs are one of very first lures I can remember using. They are essentially nothing more than a J-hook encased in a head made of lead, brass or composite material. There are lots of styles, weights, and colors, and they are essential for just about all kinds of fishing, especially when using soft plastic swimming lures.

The two styles that I recommend the most are boxing glove and stand-up. Both of these shapes can move across the bottom, avoiding a great many snags from grass, small rocks, and crevasses—an important feature when kids are learning to use artificial lures.

The boxing-glove style is most often used when hopping a soft plastic

Assortment of lead jig heads. The gold one is a boxing glove and the yellow one on the right is a stand-up.

grub or imitation shrimp across the bottom. When they land on the bottom the boxing-glove shape makes a nice puff of sand or mud that attracts both redfish and pompano.

The stand-up jig comes into play under popping corks. It's thinner and glides downward with a slight side-to-side wiggle after popping the cork. This motion is irresistible to seatrout, jacks, and ladyfish.

The all-around best color to use is chartreuse or yellow. You'll find many anglers in agreement with an old fishing adage, "If it ain't chartreuse, it ain't no use." From my experience this is generally right on the money; however, there's another fishing saying, "Dark colors on dark days, light colors on light days." This too is valid, so I break the chartreuse rule on overcast days by going with purple, red-, or brown jig heads.

The reasoning behind the different shades of color has to do with the fact that many fish species tend to look upward when hunting for food. On sunny days the baitfish will appear silvery and on cloudy days, shadowed. This is good to remember when selecting the colors to use when not only tying on jig heads, but also for artificial lures and soft plastics in general.

I have a special request. Please do all of us old anglers a favor. Pass these two sayings along to youngsters who hopefully will eventually share it with their children and grandchildren. These are two fishing tips that should never be lost to time.

When first introducing lead-head jigs to kids, it's best to use live shrimp as bait. Yes, this is sort of an artificial live bait combo, but it helps immensely with the prospect of a bite. Just feeling the strike of a fish, hit or miss, will inspire a youngster to keep at it.

The jig head is also a great learning tool for three of the most important aspects of fishing—casting, retrieval, and movement of an artificial bait. The redundancy of casting will improve a child's targeting aim. Retrieval will impress upon them the need to vary speeds to initiate strikes for either active or non-active fish. Movement is all about the stop and go of a retrieve. Kids will soon find out that completely stopping a retrieve will sometimes elicit a huge unexpected strike.

Keep using this combo as long as needed. Some kids will figure all three tactics out in a fishing trip or two. Some will take longer. It's up to you to figure out when it's time for them to take the next step—removing that live shrimp and replacing it with a soft plastic lure.

Soft Plastic Lures

There are literally thousands of soft plastic baits available for fishing. They come in shapes of small fish, worms, grubs, shrimp, crabs, lizards, frogs, and even some that are unidentifiable. There also seems to be hundreds of colors. Just keep the light-dark rule in mind when choosing.

While there are quite a few good starter soft plastic lures for kids in the saltwater realm my personal recommendations would be either Berkley's Gulp! Alive! Saltwater Shrimp or D.O.A. Shrimp. Both of these manufacturers have been around for a very long time and both of their soft plastic lures are proven fish catchers.

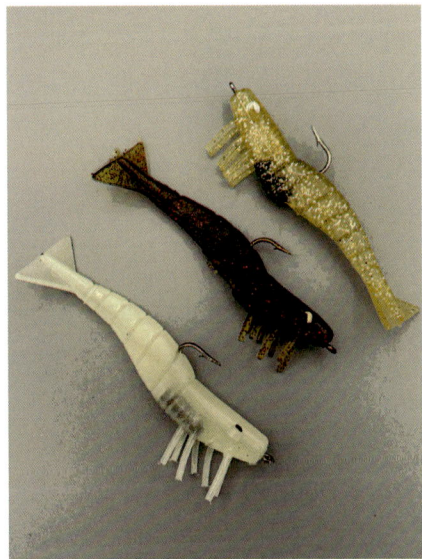

Gulp! Shrimp on the left and D.O.A. Shrimp on the right.

Gulp! Shrimp might be a tad better for kid use, as they come pre-soaked in a special liquid that gives them a smell all their own that fish can't seem to resist. The soft plastic lures must be kept in the juice they are sold in and never left to dry out on a jig head or hook at the end of the day. The unusual material stays very soft while fishing, but turns to leather when dried, which makes the lure next to impossible to remove from a hook or jig a day later. Also, do NOT, under any circumstances, open the package in the house. Their odor is disliked by everyone except fish.

When it comes to size and color, start out with the three-inch New Penny. Place it on the appropriate-colored lead-head jig and then have the youngster cast it out. Once in the water tell the child to let it sink a bit and then slowly retrieve it while giving the tip of the rod a slight small jerk every so often. Be sure to tell them to vary the speed and the amount of action until they figure out what works best to get the fish to strike at the lure.

As time passes, the youngsters can expand their arsenal of soft plastics. Take them to a tackle shop and let them pick out a few that they think might work. I used to do this on my boat during charters. I had an assorted box of soft plastics that I'd let kids pick from. They were not only allowed to fish with it; they could also keep them to take home if they wished. If they caught a fish with it I'd make sure to take a photo with that lure showing from the corner of the fishes' mouth. Either way it was a win with the youngest kids. They love catching fish and they love trinkets and souvenirs.

Hard-Body Lures

Graduating to hard-body artificial lures is the next step and using them depends on the child's age and maturity. Most hard baits carry from one to three treble hooks that could possibly make them a bit dangerous for the youngest anglers. I'll leave it to the parents to make this decision.

Hard-body lures can be made of plastic, hard rubber or wood and come in many styles and colors. Most are made to look like a baitfish and can be retrieved with either a steady reeling action or an erratic reel and jerk combination. I've found the easiest ones for kids to start with are those that only need to be reeled in at various speeds. They are traditionally called lipped artificial lures. The lip is a small spoon-like appendage that sticks out of the front of the lure so that when retrieved the lip causes the lure to wiggle from side to side. The lip can also serve double duty in that it will also cause the lure to dive deeper in the water, depending on how fast it's retrieved.

Yo-Zuri Chrystal Minnows are one of the most popular lipped hard baits.

Most lipped artificials can be purchased in versions of floating, suspending, and sinking. The floating is recommended as a starting point. If the youngster reels too fast and the lure hits bottom, the reeling action can be stopped, and in most cases the lure will slowly rise back to the surface. This rising motion will also cause fish to strike the lure if this technique is used as a tactic while retrieving. A small stop, and then the rise of the lure is irresistible to many gamefish.

The suspending lure is designed to stay in the middle depths of the water column. Once cast it will sink two or three feet deep and stay there unless retrieved quickly. It will then dive down just like the floater. It will also rise when reeling is halted, but at a much slower rate than the floating lure. The suspending lure is best used for fish that like to cruise back country grass flats in middle depths of five to six feet of water.

This sinking lure is as advertised by its name. Once cast it will slowly sink to the bottom and stay there even when retrieving stops. When it comes to kids learning to fish, this would be the last choice on the list unless you plan on fishing nearshore waters greater than five feet deep over a sandy bottom. If used you'll want to make sure there are very few if any snags on the bottom; otherwise the lure may be lost with a break off.

There are far too many manufactures to list them all, so here are just a few that I've used while fishing with kids that pass the muster.

The MirrOlure L29MR has been around for a very long time and still outshines a great many of its competitors. The pointed shape makes it easy to cast and it has a nice wiggle when retrieved.

The Yo-Zuri 3D Crystal Minnow is amazing. They are well-made and come in a host of color combinations. The floating version is quite buoyant and will rise a bit faster than other lures when retrieving is stopped. They come with seriously sharp hooks that hold up well in saltwater, but also require special safety attention with children in the younger age group.

Rapala has been making lures as long as I can remember. Their Saltwater X-Rap is a favorite of mine. At this writing they are only available in suspending versions, but if the retrieve is halted they will float back up into the water column. However, you can't beat the wiggle. Almost no action needs to be imparted by the angler that will make this lure any more attractive to a fish.

When it comes to picking colors for artificial hard baits, go with what looks natural. Most saltwater baitfish have silver sides and their backs are usually black, blue, or green. I'm personally partial to any shade of green from very light to very dark. However, if small finger mullet is a normal species found where you like to fish, going with a black back is a much better match-the-hatch decision.

Poppers

Simply put, a popper-style lure is very similar to a popping cork, but with hooks added. They float on the surface and come with a cupped face designed to make noise when suddenly pulled on by jerking the rod tip. The noise and splash they make are a big-time fish attractor. They are simple to use and elicit a fish strike like no other lure. Kids seem to love using them because of the visual payoff they get when a fish crashes through the surface of the water to strike the bait. Poppers also have an unusual posi-

The Chug Bug has been a part of fishing for many years and kids love to use it to catch fish.

tive trait. If the fish or angler misses the strike with an errant hook set, the fish will almost always strike again, and again, just as long as the retrieval continues. With kids this is priceless. A swing and a miss is often rewarded with an immediate second try.

There are lots of poppers on the market, but one of the best is an old-ie-but-goodie. I was first introduced to the *Storm's Rattlin' Chug Bug* while fishing years ago for bass on freshwater lakes in Kentucky. After moving back to Florida in the early 1990s I discovered there was a saltwater version. Of course an old freshwater *Chug Bug* could be used, but the salt would ruin it after only a few fishing trips. To this day it's still one of the standard lures I continue to use when hunting for seatrout on shallow water grass flats.

Kids love fishing with *Chug Bugs*. There's nothing better than a lure that pops when pulled and then proceeds to get crushed on the surface with a fish strike. Kids actually laugh with delight when this happens. Better still, as I mentioned earlier, if the fish comes unbuttoned and the youngster begins popping the lure once again, the odds are very good that the same fish, or another, will attack it.

Artificial Lures for Freshwater

This chapter begins with exactly the same introduction on safety as the saltwater artificial lure chapter. If you've already read the saltwater version please go ahead and read it again. I believe you can't say enough about fishing safely with youngsters.

First and foremost, here's a safety tip for the use of artificial lures when used by children and in most cases with adults, too. Be sure to flatten down the hook barbs. This will make removing a hook from human skin much easier if the unexpected happens.

The barb of a fishing hook is the small appendage near the tip of the hook that helps hold the hook in place while fighting a fish. It will do the same if it penetrates human skin. However, human skin is much tougher than that of most fish, so it's quite difficult and painful to remove a hook that has entered the skin deep enough to go past the barb. Flattening, or mashing down the barb, is easy to do and will make releasing a human much easier. A pair of needle-nose pliers is all that's needed to take care of the barb, and in no way will this affect the integrity of the hook itself.

My general rule is to remove the barbs only on artificial lures that have the more typical treble hooks. A great many of these same lures have at least two trebles, and sometimes three. As mentioned, the barb is designed to help hold the hook in the mouth of a fish. I honestly believe that most anglers, even children, will have a hard time losing a hooked fish with at least three hooks in the mouth.

Rubber Worms

I believe that the best way to teach artificial lure fishing to a youngster in the freshwater realm is to begin with soft plastic worms. This is an observation based on years of watching kids fish in lakes, small streams, and canals in Florida. If they aren't using some form of live bait they are most likely using a soft plastic worm, lizard, or frog. I'm guessing this path is

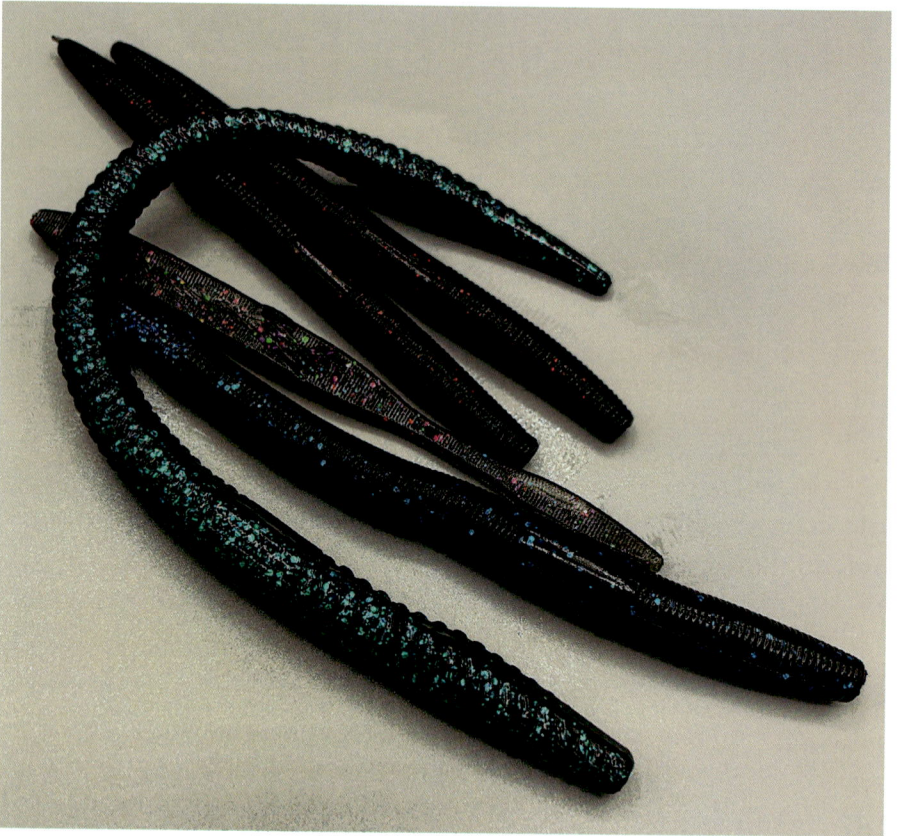

An assortment of soft plastic worms used for freshwater fishing.

taken because these selections work better than all the others, and there are an absolute ton of other choices.

I asked a friend of mine who guides and fishes Lake Okeechobee this very question not long ago. Why artificial worms? His answer wasn't at all what I expected. He said, "Because they are cheap." Seriously? Yep, that was the gist of it, but he added that it's also because there are zillions of different sizes and shapes available along with many, many color variations.

When it comes to kids learning to fish saving money by using less expensive lures is a good thing, because they are going to lose artificial lures at a fairly quick pace. That's a given, so you might as well start them with something that doesn't cost too much and, oh by the way, also works.

Hooks and Soft Plastics

Before jumping into soft plastics, let's talk about hooks. There are also zillions of these too, so I'll start with the oldest and still most popular, the offset worm hook. I've included a photo because I've discovered it's really hard to describe these without one.

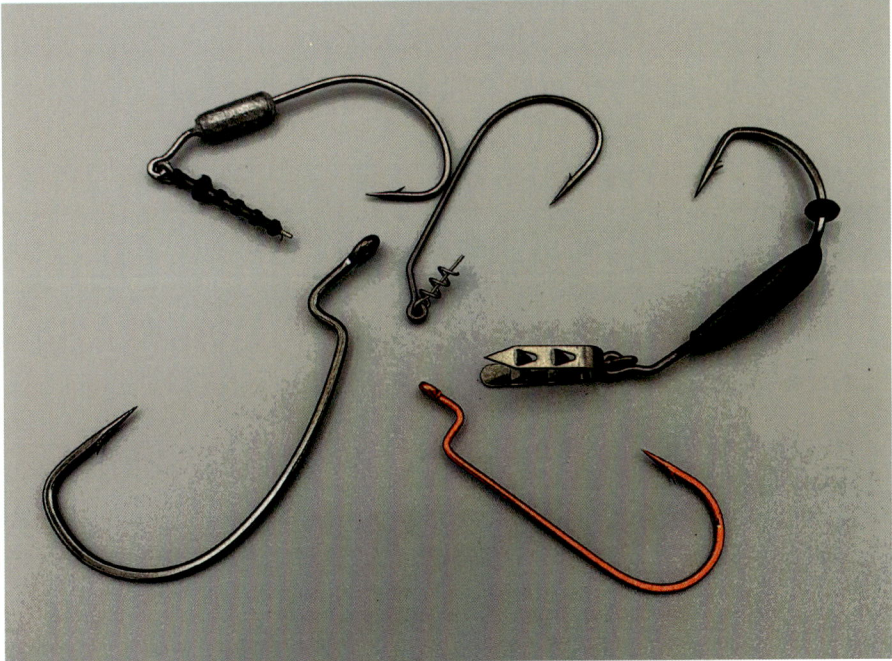

Offset hooks come in a variety of styles including clips, weighted and twist screws.

Offset worm hooks are essential to fishing soft plastics in freshwater and saltwater. Once rigged correctly they will allow long skinny baits, like worms, to hang naturally and not have any bumps or kinks. This is important to making the lure look real to highly alert gamefish.

When bass fishing with a hook and worm my favorite hook is an offset Owner in sizes 2/0 to 5/0. I'll use light wire for finesse fishing and heavy wire if I believe that a monster bass may be hanging out in tall grass or thick lily pads.

When it comes to kids I'd start with a 2/0 offset worm hook, a 7-inch worm with a flat "wavy" tail, and either Junebug or Watermelon as the color of choice. This is my go-to. It works in just about all kinds of water quality conditions and on both sunny and overcast days. Sure, there are lots and lots of other combinations, but this will at least give you a starting point for teaching a youngster how to fish artificials in freshwater.

A good tip to give kids when they are starting out with soft plastic worms is to be sure to slow down. Work the worm throughly and take your time with the retrieve. Worms in real life move slowly and are prone to hiding in deep grass or in riprap along the sides of a lake or canal. It's very important to make the worm lure look like the real thing. Slowing down will help get the job done.

As the learning curve increases, the world of soft plastics can be added to and adjusted. Next in line would be lizards, an essential lure in Florida in the summer months, along with frogs. These two creatures grow in population once the rainy season begins so it makes sense to add them to the soft plastic lure arsenal. Colors can be experimented with as well as different types of worm bodies and lengths. The possibilities are almost endless.

Freshwater Poppers

In saltwater the natural progression for kids learning to fish artificials is usually a jump from soft plastics to hard bodied lures. However, I've found that in the freshwater world it's actually better to go to topwater, at least in Florida where water temperatures work well for using a topwater lure almost year round.

The *Arbogast Hula Popper* is just about as old as me, and that's saying something. This is a freshwater bass catching favorite among all anglers of all ages. Its's similar to the *Chug Bug* and the *Surface Walker* that are used in saltwater, but the design is made to imitate a frog instead of a baitfish. It has the classic scooped-out face, a round head and an hourglass-shaped body. Added to the tail-end of the lure is a skirt of rubber that resembles a hula skirt. If you're looking for a topwater lure to teach a youngster the art of working a popper in freshwater, this one would be hard to beat. My personal favorite color is green with a black striped back and a dark yellow underbelly. I can't begin to count the amount of bass I've caught while using this color combination.

The Hula Popper imitation frog popper. Note the cupped mouth and the added hula skirt.

Once again this is a lure that needs to be worked slowly and deliberately. Older kids shouldn't have an issue with the slowdown tactic, but it can be a problem with younger children, whose patience levels can be a bit lower. You'll have to make a decision on the maturity level of the youngster you're working with before moving forward with this lure stage.

Hard-Body Lures

In the world of bass fishing the hard-body lure is often referred to as a crankbait. They have a somewhat rounded body, a front lip and a couple of treble hooks. The are designed to be "cranked" by reeling in the line at

Yo-Zuri Rattl'n Vibe is a very popular artificial lure. Kids don't have to apply action, just reel at various speeds.

a certain rate of speed to elicit a strike from a largemouth bass. They are a great starter artificials for kids because it's not really necessary to put a lot of action on the lure while retrieving it. You can add stop and go action, but that's easy for young anglers to understand and do well.

Freshwater fishing also uses hard-body baits that are shaped like baitfish and retrieved in many different ways. Some are stop and go while others are fished erratically with jerks of the rod tip while being retrieved. Occasional speed increases and decreases can also be added for even more action. Young kids can have a difficult time mastering this type of artificial lure, so I'd recommend sticking with the popper or the crankbait until they show interest in moving up to more complicated retrieve techniques. Please, always remember to keep it simple for kids that are just starting out. The less frustration they have the more likely they'll continue to enjoy the sport of fishing.

Fish Species—Saltwater

As I mentioned in the very first chapter of this book, young children tend to have a shorter attention span than older kids and adults. Well, some adults. You know who you are.

When it comes to species of fish to target while fishing with kids it's important to keep it simple at first. As the child gains interest they will most likely ask this question. "Where can we catch bigger fish?" That's a clue that it's time to move up to the more difficult and larger gamefish. However, take your time. If you try to push this too early the patience of a child may wane and so will their interest in angling.

There are several good choices of saltwater species to focus on when introducing youngsters to fishing. Mangrove snapper, spotted seatrout, and ladyfish are all good, but each of these has a minimum beginning age limit where they work best, so I'll take them in order from the youngest potential angler to the somewhat older.

Mangrover Snapper

The abundance of mangrove snapper, both inshore and nearshore, makes them my first choice when there's a brand-new young angler fishing from a boat. I often refer to them as the freshwater bluegill of the sea. They can be targeted year round in Florida, except on the very coldest winter days, and even then there's a chance of finding them well into the backcountry soaking up warmth in the late-day sun.

Inshore mangrove snapper love to hang out near mangrove shorelines (thus the name) and islands with heavy overhanging branches. They also love the cover of blowdowns—broken mangrove branches that have fallen into the water. While most of the snapper will be below the slot limit of ten inches in length (at this writing), there will almost always be a few big ones mixed in.

Offshore, they can be found in a wide range of water depths. With young kids do your best to stay in waters less than thirty to thirty-five

Offshore mangrove snapper will almost always be bigger than the inshore version.

feet deep. A combination of offshore current and winds can make it very difficult to feel the bite in deeper water. Mangrove snapper are most often found on small rock piles, and on open areas of hard bottom that have a mix of loose rocks and small ledges which they love to hide in to ambush smaller fish.

In either case, once located, the bite will be constant until every single one of them has been hooked or landed. They never seem to give up. One thing I've noticed while targeting snapper is the smaller fish tend to go for the bait first while the larger ones seem to be waiting in cover. Perhaps this caution is how the bigger ones got bigger.

At some point the bite will slow down and come to a stop. A move to another nearby location should start things right back up again. Mangrove snapper are very "location" oriented and tend to hang in the same area day after day, week after week, so they can be fairly easy to find on repeated fishing trips.

Rigging for Mangrove Snapper

The first of two tackle options can be used for inshore or offshore. It's a simple rig, made out of nothing more than a small hook, a lightweight split shot, and a chunk of fresh shrimp. Drop it to the bottom near the mangrove and get ready for almost instant nibbling and full-on bites. Line sizes can also be fairly lightweight. I use a fifteen-pound test braided line combined with a twenty-pound test fluorocarbon leader. Both of these recommendations are heavier than needed for mangrove snapper, but you never know when the big surprise will come along, especially offshore, so it's nice to be prepared for that eventuality.

I'd suggest using a small number 1 or 1/0 circle hook. The circle style hook sets itself so youngsters don't have to do anything but reel when a bite is felt. It also works well to offset the bait stealing abilities of mangrove snapper.

Split-shot size should be a number four, three or two with the two being the heaviest. Yes, that's one of those weird backwards fishing numbering schemes. The more current in the area you're fishing, the more weight will be needed.

The second rig is for inshore and involves all of the above with the addition of a popping cork used as a simple bobber. If you find that the young angler is having trouble detecting a bite, adding a bobber will make hooking fish a lot easier. I don't encourage using a bobber as a first tackle setup because it's very important to teach a child the art of feeling a bite over watching a cork disappear. However, avoiding frustration on a youngster's early fishing trips is a must, so do what you have to do when necessary.

The size of the cork should be larger than your typical red and white round plastic bobber. I'd recommend the larger styrofoam egg-shaped ones, and be sure to use a color that's easy to see up against the mangrove. Bright orange would be a good choice. Yellow and chartreuse are also available, but those colors tend to blend into the mangrove background, especially at a distance or in dim light.

When using either tackle setup be sure to keep the shrimp bait offer-

This nice spotted seatrout is almost as big as the kids!

ing small. I never recommend using a whole live shrimp when fishing for mangrove snapper. Small pieces work best and also force the fish to grab the entire chunk instead of nibbling the bait off the hook until it's gone.

Spotted Seatrout

For young anglers over eight years of age, seatrout is an excellent species to target. This abundant saltwater fish is found in many locations across the state of Florida including open grass flats, passes, beaches, nearshore Gulf-waters and the entrances of many saltwater creeks and rivers. They bite well year round and also keep eating in cooler winter weather, even when water temperatures are in the 60s. I don't suggest searching for them with kids in tow, especially in places you've never fished before. Instead, concentrate on areas where you've already located seatrout in the past and have had some regular success in that area.

As kids get a bit older and more patient, fishing for seatrout is a great way to teach the art of paying attention to other wildlife in order to find fish. Seatrout are often found on open grass flats where there's an abundance of baitfish and other wildlife, such as terns, gulls, osprey, and dolphins. Showing kids the relationships between these different species, and telling them why they are all in the same area to feed, will encourage them to pay attention to signs that might otherwise be missed.

Be sure to point out the schools of small baitfish that drift across the flats. Called "rain bait" by fishing guides, these small anchovies create a disturbance on the water's surface that looks like a mini rainstorm. I change the name when I'm fishing with kids to "trout candy" since every child knows how good candy can be.

Rigging for Spotted Seatrout

Start with a popping cork rig as the first choice of terminal tackle. This setup will actually be the beginning of teaching a young angler how to cast and how to use an artificial lure even though this rig is more commonly used with live bait.

The popping cork is a tool that can draw fish to your bait offering by using a sound that fish are familiar with. The cork, when sharply pulled by a quick motion of the fishing rod, will make a noise that sounds like gamefish hitting bait near the surface of the water. This distinct sound will bring other gamefish from a good distance away to partake in what they believe their buddies are eating. Working the rod in combination with the reel and learning when to pop slowly or quickly are all positive ways to teach kids how to eventually use artificial lures.

Seatrout can be a bit leader-shy, meaning they are more likely to see or sense visible fishing line when used as a leader between the cork and the hook. I'd highly recommend using fluorocarbon instead of monofilament fishing line as a leader. Fluorocarbon essentially disappears in water and is also less susceptible to abrasion and sharp objects. The length of the leader will vary based on the depth of the water being fished. On average, three to four feet is a good starting point since most seatrout like feeding in a depth of that range.

Finish the rig with a 1/0 to 3/0 circle hook and a small split-shot weight placed on the leader line about six inches above the hook. The most common size split shot is a number two which weighs about 1/4 ounce. To that add at least a half of a shrimp for bait. Fisherman have long argued whether the head or the tail gets more bites. Trust me, both work well, especially for hungry fish.

Once landed, seatrout can be safely handled by youngsters. While they do have some nasty-looking fangs, they are mostly harmless as the trout doesn't have much jaw pressure. The fangs are actually used to capture bait and then with a head shake, the bait is quickly eaten.

Ladyfish

These abundant mini tarpon-like fish are exiting to catch, even for adults. Very young children will have a problem keeping them hooked up and may grow easily frustrated if a lot of them are missed or pop off the hook before a photo can be taken. However, if you are introducing a youth to fishing who's eight to ten years old, I believe you're good to go. The constant hookups should make up for any fish lost during battles.

A little lady with a BIG ladyfish!

One of the best locations to start a hunt for ladyfish is the Gulf side openings of any pass that connects a bay to the Gulf of Mexico. Most of these openings have sandy bottoms with fairly shallow sand flats just outside the deeper channel. Ladyfish love to chase baitfish on the sand flats in roughly four to six feet of water. The clearer the water the better;

however, I've caught plenty of them in water that has been clouded up due to heavy winds.

Rigging for Ladyfish

The best bet for catching ladyfish is once again the popping cork rig set up exactly the same way it would be for spotted seatrout. The only difference is the cork can be popped and moved more quickly. Ladyfish are aggressive feeders, so quick movements work best.

As I mentioned earlier, this will be the first step toward using artificial lures. Once the youngster has mastered the popping cork it's time to remove it and replace the circle hook with a lead jig head tipped with a chunk of shrimp. This move will cover three learning lessons at once... casting, setting the hook, and using something other than a plain hook to catch fish. You are now the instructor and your job is to have the patience to teach each step to the youngster.

With the removal of the popping cork a leader line will have to be tied directly to the fishing line. That's going to require a line-to-line knot. Uh-oh. Now it's time to teach the young angler a knot or two. It may be best to do this at home, but the sooner you do it, the better. Believe me, kids love any additional independence they can get, and you'll be surprised how quickly they learn knot tying. I recommend that you go with one you've tied and used successfully as a starting point. After they've mastered that one move on to a few others.

Lead-head jigs come in many sizes and lots of colors. For catching ladyfish I'd go with chartreuse, yellow, or white, in that order. Hook sizes can range from 1/0 to 3/0 with weights of one-quarter or three-eighths of an ounce. The weight choice is made based on water depth, currents, and wind. Shallow depths mixed with light winds and currents calls for a light-weight rig. The opposite is true for deeper water with more current and winds. It's a balancing act where sometimes experimentation is needed to get the best results. Color also comes into play with the above conditions. Chartreuse can be seen better in deeper water than yellow or white. Want to make it easy? Just stick with chartreuse.

A nice-sized seatrout caught near Sanibel Island in Pine Island Sound.

After casting, the youngster will have to move the jig with short jerks of the rod tip while occasionally letting the jig drop all the way to the bottom. When the strike is felt it's time to set the hook. This will be another new learning experience since up until now, circle hooks that required no hook set have been in use.

Ladyfish almost always jump like crazy when hooked. They'll spin, twirl, and even tail walk. Care must be taken when going after these silvery fish because their antics tend to dislodge and throw hooks right back at anglers. I'd highly recommend some kind of eye protection—sunglasses will work—and make sure that children don't try to reach for a caught ladyfish, or just about any other saltwater gamefish, once it's brought alongside the boat or near the shoreline of the beach. A head shake can dislodge the jig, and if pressure is still on the line the jig will suddenly come directly back at them or another angler.

Kids have a bad habit, I believe due to the excitement of catching a fish, of reeling as hard and as fast as possible, and then suddenly jerking the fish into the boat long before the fish is even slightly worn out. A freshly caught ladyfish jumping around in a boat, on the beach, or on a dock is very likely to dislodge the jig on their own. The hook can easily wind up in a hand or other body part which will make for a very bad fishing trip. As the adult, do your best to handle all of the releases until the child is old enough to understand the dangers and feels confident enough to release the fish on their own. Whenever possible, use a landing net.

When my youngest daughter began fishing she loved catching ladyfish, but was a little disturbed by their propensity to poop all over everything when one was brought into the boat. This actually cured her of the "yanking the fish into the boat" issue but at the same time more were lost at boat side. That seemed OK with her and me as well.

Be wary. Ladyfish are not very ladylike.

Fish Species—Freshwater

In my opinion the species of choice to start young anglers fishing in freshwater is by far a panfish. Specifically bluegill. These little guys are located in just about every freshwater impoundment and will readily feed year round in Florida. Sometimes called the "gateway drug" of freshwater fishing, the bluegill is easy to find and easy to catch. As a matter of fact, the first fish I ever caught while learning to fly fish was a bluegill. See what happened to me?

Bluegill

If you have a friend with a small pond or lake, start there. If not, the second best locations are the many canals that take rain runoff from the

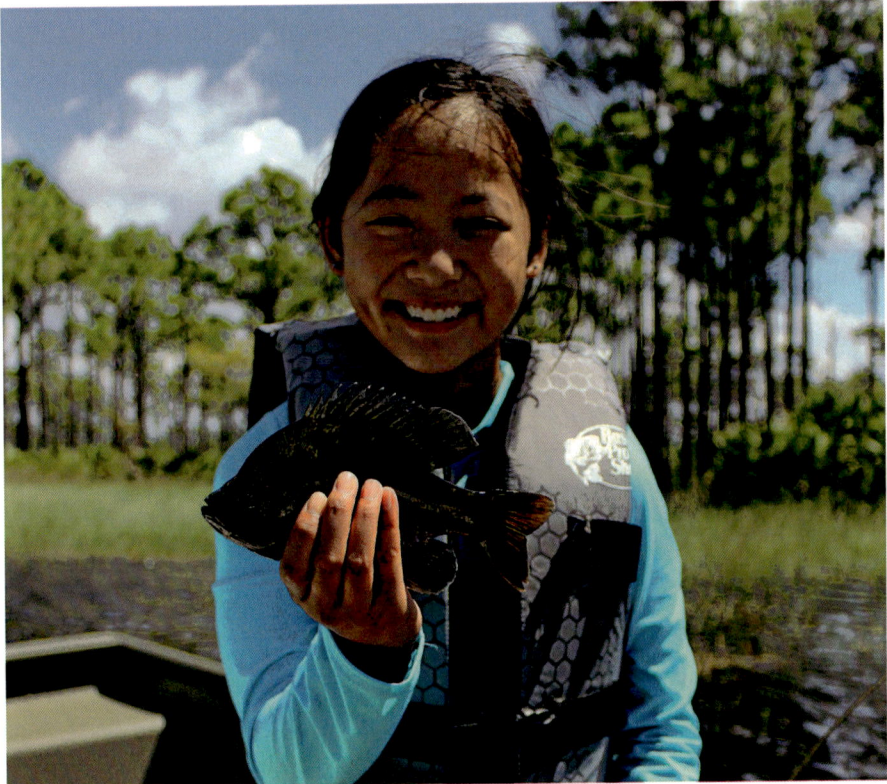

A good sized bluegill will put up a heck of fight!

mainland to the creeks and rivers that eventually spill into the bays and then onward to the Gulf of Mexico. There are also lots of parks that allow fishing in designated areas as well as access to those drainage canals.

Rigging for Bluegill

Think small and lightweight. Start kids with the classic red and white plastic bobber. Below the bobber tie on a small No. 4 brass-colored j-hook. You can also add a small split shot weight to help keep the bait low in the water column, although bluegill will feed right at the surface if the food is there. In some freshwater locations it would be a good idea to add a fluorocarbon leader on the off chance that something bigger and more exciting happens to grab the bait. Fifteen-pound test should be good to start with.

The bait can be live night crawlers, dough balls or wax worms. Of those three I far and away prefer wax worms, if you can find them at a bait shop, for catching bluegill. These small whiteish grub-like worms are durable, have an outer skin that holds up well when placed on a hook, and a bluegill will gobble them down without hesitation.

Keep tackle and lines as light as possible, but don't go too small. Just because the pond is full of small panfish doesn't mean that a big bass couldn't be swimming there, too. Always be ready for the unexpected.

Bluegill are ferocious fighters for their size and will give a youngster a tussle from the strike to the landing. They are pretty much harmless for kids to handle and they are a great teaching tool when it comes to carefully removing hooks and returning fish to the water.

Here's an important tip. A lot of young kids don't want to keep fish. They'd much rather name them, talk to them, and then return them to water. Don't worry, they'll grow into wanting to keep some of them for dinner as they get older, and that's a good time to teach them about size and bag limits along with how to properly clean and filet a fish. In the meantime, if the youngster has named the fish Nemo it would probably be best to release it.

Florida Invasives

The state of Florida has become a haven for exotic invasive fish species thanks mostly to aquarium owners dumping tropical fish they bought and no longer wanted into nearby drainage canals. African cichlids, Mayan cichlids and many species of tilapia are now established in freshwater impoundments across southern Florida. They flourish because our waters stay warm enough year round, along with the fact that there is plenty of food to eat. It's not at all unusual to hook up with lots of invasive fish, especially if you are using bait to catch bluegill.

While they may be fun to catch, they are slowly taking habitat and food away from native species. The Florida freshwater fishing regulations requires the removal of almost all non-native or invasive fish species that

Peacock bass are a top freshwater prize found in lakes and canals in the southern regions of Florida.

Largemouth bass are highly sought after by all anglers, including kids.

are caught by anglers. This can be accomplished by harvesting for food, using as cut bait, or being disposed of. Keep in mind that there are some non-native species, such as peacock bass, that were put in Florida waters with the purpose of controlling other fish populations. Check the freshwater regulations carefully before permanently removing any fish from the water.

The cichlid varieties are a blast to catch. While a little more finicky than bluegill, they fight very much like saltwater gamefish. They'll run drag off the reel, make sudden turns and long runs at a moment's notice. Make sure to be careful when removing hooks. Most cichlids have small, sharp teeth and spines on their fins and bodies.

Largemouth Bass

It probably won't take long for the child you're fishing with to start asking about catching bigger fish. That's where largemouth bass come into play. While they may seem somewhat easy to target, they can be one of the most finicky fish in freshwater. The good news is they like live bait a lot, specifically shiners (minnows).

Bass can be found along the edge of ponds that have a steep drop-off. They also use overhanging branches for shade and feed near points that fall away to deeper water. When fishing canals look for areas where rock boulders and riprap have been placed to protect banks from water erosion. The rocks hold bait and small critters that bass love to eat.

Drainage pipes are also a good location for bass hunting, especially after a steady rain. They also like to hang underneath lily pads in open water areas. Dropping a bait as close as possible to either of these locations will almost always get a look and a bite.

Rigging for Largemouth Bass

The best tackle for beginners is a hook and bobber combination with a nice fresh, live shiner. Bass have a hard time ignoring a little fish for dinner, and if it's placed in the right location the strike should come almost immediately.

Circle hooks can be used to catch bass while using live shiners, but they've never reached the same popularity they have for saltwater fishing. This may be because of the abundance of artificial soft plastic baits used for bass fishing, that require some kind of J-hook. Also, the mouth of a largemouth bass can be tough, so a circle hook may not set up properly.

Since the need for J-hooks is fairly prevalent, introducing a youngster to bass fishing would also be a good time to begin instruction on properly setting a hook when a bite is felt.

Big-time hook sets have long been the traditional way bass are caught. If you watch as many fishing shows as I have you'll soon figure out that the monster hook set is a big part of the game. When the bass eats a bait it will hold on to it for a few seconds. The angler will wind in a bit of slack line while at the same time lower the tip of the rod toward the fish. When the line comes tight the angler sets the hook with a huge over-the-shoulder hook set. I'm always amazed that rod tips aren't broken on a regular basis in the world of bass fishing.

Once hooked and landed, bass can be held by its mouth (lipped) and hoisted out of the water. In other words, you don't really need a net when retrieving a caught bass. You can simply grab its lower lip with your thumb in the mouth and your fingers on the chin and then lift.

If a lure is being used with multiple treble hooks there's a chance of becoming accidentally attached to the bass if you try the lipping method. Not good. Especially with kids. It would be a much better and safer idea to use a long-handled landing net.

Please note: The state of Florida has alligators in just about every freshwater impoundment. It's not advised to lean down along the water's edge to retrieve a fish by hand, or to release one the same way. Lowering your profile is an open invitation for a gator to make its move and lunge toward its target. The use of a long-handled net is advised when landing any fish near the water's edge. After removing the hook I'd recommend a simple toss for returning the fish to the water.

Fishing Locations for Kids

This book is focused on saltwater and freshwater fishing in the state of Florida. The following locations are what I believe to be good starting points for youngsters who are just beginning their fishing adventures. However, there are infinite places to fish in the United States, so I believe it's possible to relate some of the Florida locations recommended to locations in other parts of the U.S.

Inland Florida

From the northern Florida state line all the way south to the Florida Keys, there are lots of great fishing venues located inland from the Atlantic Ocean and the Gulf of Mexico. Some are small farm ponds, and others are as big as Lake Okeechobee, the second largest inland lake in the continental United States, and the largest in Florida. There are also a great many beautiful springs that can be fished in central Florida as well as rivers and small streams.

Some of my favorite places to freshwater fish are the canals and drainage ditches that move rainwater from inland Florida all the way to the coasts. They are everywhere, and most have fairly easy on-foot access and hold an amazing array of fresh, and sometimes even saltwater, fish.

Ditch Fishing

Travis Palmer, a fishing friend of mine, coined this name years ago as a way of identifying one of his favorite fishing locations. This mostly saltwater fisherman showed me a fun way to catch lots of interesting freshwater species without having to own a boat, kayak, or canoe.

The runoff canals we fished were located in central Lee County near Fort Myers, Florida, but I can assure you they are located just about everywhere in the state. Florida, in general, receives a lot of rain, especially in the summer months, and that rainwater runoff has to go somewhere.

The catches from these drainage ditches included several varieties of cichlids along with tilapia, bluegill, bass, peacock bass, and even small tarpon and snook, both of which are technically saltwater species. For bait we used everything from live shiners and nightcrawlers to artificial lures. The best thing about ditches and canals, besides good access, is there are almost always fish located there that are willing to eat. Keep in mind that because the ditches are used for rainwater drainage, fishing them during the dry season can be more of challenge than during the rainy season. One of the best times to go ditch fishing is right after the first couple of rainy weeks in early summer. The bite then is what fishing dreams are made of.

Parks

All across Florida, and in a great many states, there are public, state, and national parks that allow fishing. Before going be sure to either check the park's rules online or give them a call and ask about access specifically for fishing.

As an example, Huge Taylor Birch State Park, located in Fort Lauderdale, Florida, doesn't permit freshwater fishing in the lakes and small ponds in the park. However, they do allow saltwater fishing from the seawall that runs along the Intracoastal Waterway on the western boundary of the park.

It's also a good idea to check opening and closing hours as most parks regulate openings based on sunrise and sunsets throughout the year.

Ponds

If you're lucky enough to know someone with a small farm or acreage that might have a pond or lake, be sure to impose upon them. Many landowners have lakes that are overrun with species that they'd like to see gone if at all possible, especially if invasive species have taken over what used to be a great bass catching lake. Don't be afraid to ask, and also let the owner know that you'll clean up after yourself and leave nothing but footprints. When I lived in Kentucky I fished in quite a few farm ponds and the catches of bass were truly amazing.

Beaches

The state of Florida has 1,350 miles of coastline. This is far and away the easiest access to fishing, and a big time fish catching location. Most beachside state parks allow fishing from their beaches, but again you'll need to check with each individual location. There are some beaches that are heavily occupied by beachgoers there to catch some sun instead of fish, so they may be off limits to anglers.

When going beach fishing it's always best to get there early. No matter where you go you'll eventually run into those that are sunning, shelling, or just walking the beach on a beautiful morning. In this case the early bird really does get the worm, and the fish.

Fishing Piers

Coastal fishing piers are very popular with all anglers and a good place to take kids fishing. There are a multitude of species that can be caught from very small to very large. Because of the continuous fishing at piers many fish hang out around them and are quick to take an offered bait.

A good many pay fishing piers don't require fishing licenses. The license is included with the price of admission. While kids in Florida can fish any-where without one up until reaching 16 years of age, it's one less thing that you'll have to worry about.

When fishing with a youngster at a pier, one of the nice side effects is the amount of fishing tips they'll receive from other fisher folks. A trip to a fishing pier is a social event where most everyone loves to talk fishing, and where you and your youngster will glean a lot of useful bait, tackle, and general fishing information.

Other States

I lived in Louisville, Kentucky, off and on for over 10 years. While there I was taken under the wing by another avid fisherman. Garry taught me the ways of freshwater creek fishing, which was quite an eye opener for this saltwater angler. We spent a lot time fishing small creeks between the cities of Louisville and Lexington, and caught a lot of fish.

Creeks are a wonderland for kids. There is much more to see there than just fish. The woods are populated with lots of birds, butterflies and deer. There are also turtles, rabbits, and other small wildlife along the creek. I have to be honest. If my first fishing trips were in the babbling creeks of Kentucky as a child, that would have thoroughly addicted me to the sport.

I use Kentucky only as an example because I'm most familiar with freshwater fishing in that state. There are many, many other similar locations all across America where wetting a line will be fun and educational for youngsters. Your adult instructional job is to find those places and take a kid fishing there.

Making Memories

When I was teaching fishing classes for Collier County Adult Education in Naples, Florida, I found there was a need to include fishing photography instruction. This came about because of the increased use of cellphones for taking outdoor sporting photos. When it came to fishing the results weren't always that great. I think part of the problem seemed to be a timing thing. In other words, anglers were anxious about returning a caught fish quickly to the water to enhance the fish's survival chances. That's a noble thing to do, but I'm sure a great many mediocre photos of some beautiful fish never made it to a frame on a desk, or to the kitchen refrigerator door.

Here's a fairly simple solution. Keep the fish in the water until you are ready to take the photo.

Fish Holders

A fish holder is a device that safely attaches to the mouth of the fish, also known as fish grippers. One of mylong time favorites is the BogaGrip. It comes in several sizes with an extremely accurate weigh scale and is made of stainless steel so it can endure repeated uses in saltwater. It's costly, but well worth the price. I've had the same one for almost 15 years!

Landing Nets

Another essential item for making great fishing photos is a quality landing net. I used the word quality on purpose. Cheaper nets are usually made of a waxed string, or a very heavy fishing line with small knots to form the net. These can be rough on fish scales and skin and eventually will rub the slime off a fish. The slime, while gross to a lot of kids, is actually very important to the health of the fish. It protects it from parasites, nicks and cuts that a fish might receive before being returned to the water.

There are newer nets that are made of a rubbery material that is smooth and formed as one piece with no knots. Not only does this material help keep the fish slime in place; it also resists the entanglement of hooks. When it comes to photographing kids with fish I'd recommend the net vs. the gripper for keeping the fish wet and alive in the water while waiting on the photography setup.

Fish Handling for Photos

Once the youngster has successfully landed the fish and high-fives all around have been given, keep the catch in the landing net and then place the net back in the water with just enough water coverage to keep the fish wet and oxygenated. When the photographer is ready with camera in hand and settings set, bring the fish in the boat, take it out of the net and pose. Wet, very much alive fish make a much better photo than a dry colorless almost dead one.

Note: See the chapter Regulations and Safe Handling for additional information.

This method can also be used even if the plan is to keep the fish for dinner. I've never been much of a fan of fish photos at the dock of an obviously dead fish that's been in a cooler of ice for the past several hours. It usually looks dead and colorless and the skin will have splotches from the ice. Many fish have fantastic colorations, so make sure to show those off by taking those prized photos shortly after the fish is landed.

Some kids have a problem with handling fish. This isn't a boy vs. girl thing. I've seen both sexes have issues with slime, teeth, and the inherent twitching and jumping of a freshly caught fish. A simple solution is the fish gripper I mentioned at the beginning of this chapter. Use it to remove the fish from the net and then pass it to the child to hold for the photograph. While this method works for holding all sizes of fish, please keep in mind that some belly support is also needed when holding larger fish.

Yes, the belly is slimy, but the internal organs of a fish are not designed to be out of the water. Organs can move and tear, and although the fish is released alive, it may soon die from those injuries. The same is true when using a gripper to hold a large fish by the mouth. The internal organ problem still exists, as well as the possibility of damaging the fish's jaws to a point where it would no longer be able to feed itself after release.

Getting the Perfect Shot

Be sure to frame the photo properly and do your best to keep extraneous items out of the background. While the fish is patiently waiting in the water, remove loose items from where the photo is going to be taken. This includes tackle, towels, sunblock tubes, water bottles, and fishing rods. One of the most distracting things found in a good many fishing photos is the inevitable rod tip sticking out of the top of the child's head in the background.

Put the sun at the back of the photographer. It's an old rule often not used by many a person. Sun behind the subject will usually make a great photo of the background, but not the fish or the child holding the fish.

If you can, remove hats and sunglasses from the kids being photographed. It's always good to see the child's smiling face. Also be sure to take

Pompano put up a heck of a fight and are a top catch for kids and adults.

LOTS of shots. It's not a film camera, so snap away from several different angles and distances.

My favorite way to take photos of youngsters is to have them stand up on the forward deck while I'm sitting on the cooler seat. The upward looking photo will enhance the sky and make for a nice background. This holds true for piers, beaches, and docks too. Simply position yourself slightly below the subject.

Remember, little things make a big difference when taking a photo that will be shared by family and friends for many years to come. Take your time setting up while the fish is in the net in the water, and then take that once-in-a-lifetime photo.

Epilogue

I've lived in many places throughout the U.S. Big cities, little towns, and now, the Florida Keys. I've seen substantial changes in the past couple of decades in the way kids are growing up. They are in a world that's a lot different than what I experienced at a very young age back in the early '60s.

When the sun came up over the horizon in the summer months my mother pushed us out the front door to play baseball in the lot across the street, build forts, tromp through the woods, fish the local ponds, and then come home when we heard the dinner bell. We drank water from garden hoses and we ate oranges from the old groves near our house.

Kids today seem to be much more concerned about their personal appearances, clicks on social media and high scores on the latest video game.

I understand that parents and grandparents today are caught in a world where it's very tough for one income to take care of an entire family. Mom and Dad both have to work to keep roofs over heads and food on tables. But a need to drop back to those earlier outside days also needs to be addressed, and soon, or our kids and grandkids are going to miss out on something amazing.

The woods, mountains, rivers, creeks, and oceans make up a much larger part of our world than anything else. Time spent in the outdoors in our youth defines how we relate to the world and the people around us.

Establishing early connections with the natural world leads us to connect with it and want to support and protect it for future generations.

My message with *Take a Kid Fishing* has long been my way of saying it's important to take kids under your wing and share with them all the wonderful things that make up the outdoors. In all the time I took kids fishing on charter trips, I never once saw a kid without a look of wonder or a smile on their faces.

Do your part. Make the extra effort to teach your kids about playing in the great outdoors before we lose a generation. That would be a travesty that I believe would be very difficult to overcome.

Remember, you can't catch a fish without a line in the water, and please, take a kid fishing.

About the Author

Captain Rob Modys is a retired Master Captain, former ESPN radio show host, popular podcaster on the Waypoint Podcast Network, and the author of two previously published books, *What I Know About Fishing Southwest Florida* and *Bridge to Paradise*. His most recent book, *Take a Kid Fishing: An Adult's Guide for Introducing Youngsters to the World of Angling*, is his third and what he feels is his most important work. "The best possible way the tradition of fishing will be carried on is if all of us adults make the effort to take a kid fishing. The great outdoors is a cure for many of the world's woes." Captain Rob lives in the Florida Keys where he's never far from the water.